Short Stack Editions | Volume 25

Avocados

by Katie Quinn

Short Stack Editions

Publisher: Nick Fauchald
Creative Director: Rotem Raffe
Editor: Kaitlyn Goalen
Copy Editor: Abby Tannenbaum
Wholesale Manager: Erin Fritch

ISBN 978-0-9975321-4-2

Printed in Virginia
January 2017

Table of Contents

Mains

Desserts

Drinks

Isn't it satisfying when something lives up to the hype?

Let's be honest: In the modern age of food, there's a new obsession every hour. And so frequently these blips on our cultural radar end up fizzling out, often because they lead to disappointment.

But avocados know what it takes to be a food-world star. They dominate the menus of hip restaurants, the hashtags of social media, the recipes of cookbooks and websites, the annals of special diets. Still, there's substance behind their hype—like the Beyoncé of ingredients, they can live up to their image by offering a cook endless paths to something delicious.

Katie Quinn is as enthusiastic an avocado fan as you can imagination, and she shamelessly buys in to some of the fruit's more marketable moments: avocado toast (check), avocado pesto with zucchini noodles (check), eggs baked in avocado halves (check). But she's also a student of global food traditions, and has expanded her research well beyond the dishes that have made this ingredient a star. She capitalizes on the avocado's fat content in recipes for pasta and compound butter; she pushes its creamy texture past the obvious (guacamole) to thicken soups and bind a mayo-less chicken salad. She even stakes the avocado's claim as an appropriate ingredient for dessert, adding richness to cupcakes and pudding.

So if you've already been swept up in avocado fever, we're happy to provide more cowbell. If you've been a skeptic, consider this the argument that helps you get on the train, once and for all. #teamavocado

—The Editors

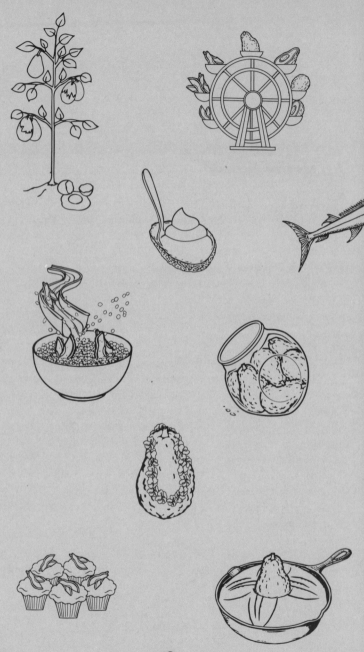

Introduction

When I was a kid growing up in Ohio, avocados were not a common ingredient in our home. They were rare and exotic. I knew they were delicious, but I rarely had the chance to eat them; for me, they might as well have been caviar.

Little did I know that avocados and I would later develop a full-blown love affair. It began with a crush: avocado toast. I ate smashed avocado on a piece of toasted 10-grain bread with a sprinkle of crushed chile flakes and a drizzle of olive oil day in and day out. My crush evolved into a relationship after I posted a video of my avocado toast recipe on my YouTube channel and my viewers enthusiastically responded—all the way from the Philippines, Brazil, Malaysia, Mexico—with suggestions of other ways I might use avocados. They described the avocado dishes that were popular in their countries, both savory and sweet, and my eyes were opened. As I worked my way through their suggestions in my kitchen, it was official: I was head over heels for avocados. I suddenly saw that avocados could be so much more than my predictable (but still delicious) avocado toast go-to.

Years later, the avocado remains a central figure in my kitchen thanks to its outstanding versatility. I can honestly say that I have never experienced avocado fatigue (even after developing recipes for this book, which involved testing approximately 130 versions of the recipes here and living off the leftovers for breakfast, lunch and dinner). I can't think of any other ingredient I'd rather have ripe in my fruit bowl at all times than avocado. Try blending avocado into a sauce, condiment or soup and it's as though you've added a nutty heavy cream. Add it to doughs and batters for its coloring and oil. Mix it with your sugary vice of choice and discover what people in Southeast Asian countries have known for centuries: Avocados belong on the sweets menu, too.

A final perk: Avocados are good for you! I'm not here to write a health book, but I love eating foods that make me feel good. Avocados top the list of foods that taste great, are filling, keep me energized and give my body 20 essential nutrients, including potassium, fiber, folate and magnesium.

In recent years, as I've built the QKatie brand of food and travel videos, my viewers have come to appreciate my frequent adoration for avocados. They comment on my videos with their own avocado recipe ideas, tag me in their avocado recipe photos and applaud quirky ways to use this fruit. (My slogan is "keep it quirky," and I think that you'll find that my penchant for thinking outside the box pays off in surprising and delicious ways.)

Finally, you can always assume that the avocados called for in each recipe should have their pits removed and skin peeled. I have omitted those instructions because it should be a given—especially for my fellow avocado enthusiasts who have picked up this book! Happy avocado-ing!

—*Katie Quinn*

Recipes

Avocado
Advice

Although there are hundreds of varieties of avocados, 80 percent of the avocados sold commercially around the world are Hass avocados, so that's what I used to test these recipes. (Plus, Hass, which has a higher fat content than others, is generally richer in flavor and more malleable for culinary purposes.)

Avocados can be differentiated many ways: A or B cultivars; Guatemalan, West Indian or Mexican seeds; green-, purple- or black-skinned. Even within each of these designations, seed size, skin color, shape, texture and flavor can vary. Hass has pebbled skin that gets progressively darker as it ripens. Green-skinned varieties tend to have smooth skin that doesn't darken as it ripens, and the flesh has less fat and therefore a more watery flavor.

Like any produce, the size of avocados at your grocery store will vary. I have found that the average Hass is about 8 ounces. The recipes in this book are hardy and can handle the slight weight differences that are sure to occur, although you can assume that when I call for 1 avocado, I am indicating 1 medium avocado. If you're still unsure, use this as a guide:

1 MEDIUM avocado	=	1 CUP cubed avocado

Cutting an Avocado

My preferred method is to cut lengthwise around the entire avocado and twist the two sides in opposite directions as I pull them apart. To remove the pit, I carefully pierce the pit with the cutting edge of my knife and twist it out. (You can also just use a spoon to scoop it out.)

Ripeness & Storing

Avocados grow on the tree for about a year before they are picked, and then they ripen off the tree. The flesh of the avocado gets creamier and tastier as it ripens. Ripe, ready-to-eat Hass avocados will yield to gentle pressure and can be dark green or purplish-black. Avoid buying avocados that feel mushy when you squeeze them gently in the grocery store, as they've probably been dropped or gone bad. You can assume that all of the recipes in this book call for ripe avocados, unless otherwise noted.

Need to speed up an avocado's ripening? Place it in a brown paper bag with a banana; bananas emit ethylene gas, which expedites the ripening process.

Once the avocados are ripe, keep them in the refrigerator if you aren't going to use them right away. A fully ripe avocado will stay good for up to a week in the refrigerator.

To store an already-cut avocado, wrap it tightly in plastic wrap or place it in an airtight container and keep in the refrigerator. To avoid further discoloration, brush the avocado flesh with lemon juice, lime juice or white vinegar.

As with all produce, avocados are best eaten in season, which is typically from March through October for Hass avocados from California.

Avocado Oil

Wherever I mention avocado oil in this book, I prefer virgin avocado oil as it's light, with a nutty and mild flavor profile.

Virgin avocado oil has a smoke point of 375° to 400°, while the smoke point of regular avocado oil is between 480° and 520°. Either style is a good choice for sautéing.

Hawaiian Fruit Salad & Pancake Breakfast

One morning during a trip to Kauai, Hawaii, I was placed in charge of breakfast for our rental house. Pancakes are an easy crowd-pleaser, especially with the trick of folding whipped egg whites into the batter, which takes the fluff factor to the next level (hat tip to my buddy J. Kenji Lopez-Alt for the technique). To round out the breakfast, I stopped by the nearest fruit stand and grabbed an armful of produce, including a large, smooth, green-skinned avocado. The following recipe is what resulted, to the acclaim of the entire house. Since apple bananas and chikoo aren't readily available outside Hawaii, substitute banana for the apple banana and kiwi for the chikoo.

For the ginger syrup:

One 5-inch knob of ginger, peeled

¾ cup turbinado sugar

For the fruit salad:

½ cup apple banana (or banana) chunks

½ cup papaya chunks

1 cup avocado chunks

½ cup chikoo (also called sapodilla) or kiwi chunks

For the kumquat cream cheese:

5 kumquats, finely chopped

1 cup cream cheese, softened

For the pancakes:

2 cups all-purpose flour

1 teaspoon baking powder

½ teaspoon baking soda

1 teaspoon kosher salt

1 tablespoon sugar

2 eggs, yolks and whites separated

2 cups buttermilk, shaken

5 tablespoons unsalted butter, melted

Coconut oil, for the pan

serves 4 to 6

Make the ginger syrup: In a small saucepan over medium heat, combine the ginger, 1 cup of water and the sugar and bring to a simmer. Remove the pan from the heat. Let it sit for at least 30 minutes, then discard the ginger and set the pan aside.

Make the fruit salad: In a large bowl, combine the apple banana, papaya, avocado and chikoo chunks. Drizzle the ginger syrup over the fruit salad and toss gently, being careful not to smush the delicate avocado and papaya. Set aside.

Make the cream cheese: In a small bowl, stir the kumquats into the cream cheese until fully incorporated. Set aside.

Make the pancakes: In a medium bowl, combine the flour, baking powder, baking soda, salt and sugar. In a separate bowl, beat the egg whites until stiff peaks form. In a third bowl, whisk the egg yolks and buttermilk together. Add the melted butter, then gently fold in the egg whites. Add that mixture to the dry ingredients and gently fold until just combined. Let the batter sit for 5 minutes so the gluten can rest and the starch molecules can absorb everything in the mix.

Heat a large heavy-bottomed nonstick pan until it's nice and hot, then put a dab of coconut oil on it and ladle on batter to make two small- to medium-size pancakes. Cook until browned on the bottom and bubbling on top, about 2½ minutes. Flip the pancakes and cook until the other side is browned, about 2 minutes longer. Transfer the pancakes to a plate and place in a warm oven while you repeat the process with the remaining pancake batter.

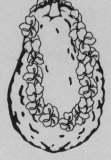

To serve, smear the cream cheese on top of the pancakes and top with the fruit salad.

Asian-Inspired Avocado Smash

I love a recipe that has an action verb in its title—it makes me feel like I'm living in a comic book. (Smash!) The three principal ingredients of an avocado smash are avocados, citrus and cheese. In Melbourne, Australia, where this is a popular brunch dish, it is served with a poached egg on top. My culinary school buddy Ryan, who is Australian, introduced me to this dish, and I tweaked it after a trip to Australia, Indonesia and Thailand, pulling inspiration from each of those countries.

2 poached eggs

4 tablespoons soy sauce

2 avocados

4 ounces feta cheese, cut into rough cubes

4 teaspoons fresh lime juice

2 teaspoons rice vinegar

Salt and freshly ground black pepper, to taste

2 tablespoons cilantro leaves, chopped

2 scallions, chopped, light and dark green parts separated

½ teaspoon finely grated ginger

2 teaspoons sesame seeds, toasted, divided

Chile-garlic sauce, for serving

4 pieces of quality whole grain bread, toasted, for serving

serves
2

This dish comes together quickly, so have your poached eggs ready and stored in warm water.

Place the soy sauce in a small saucepan and bring to a boil; reduce the heat to medium low and cook until the sauce has reduced to half its original volume, about 5 minutes. Remove from the heat and set aside.

In a medium bowl, use a fork to roughly smash the avocados. Add the feta, lime juice and rice vinegar and mix to combine. Taste the mixture and season with salt and pepper. (Since feta cheese is salty, you'll want to be shy with the salt at first and add more at the end, if desired.) Add the cilantro, the white and light green parts of the scallion (reserve the dark green slices for garnish), ginger and most of the toasted sesame seeds (reserve some for garnish). Taste and add more salt or pepper, if desired.

Transfer the avocado mixture to a shallow serving bowl and top with the poached eggs, dark green slices of scallion, reserved sesame seeds, reserved soy sauce reduction and a dash of chile-garlic sauce. Serve with the toast.

Avocado-Baked Eggs with Harissa & Garlic Yogurt

Any time I eat a spicy breakfast, I feel transported to the places that eschew bland or sweet morning meals for dishes that make you sweat. I think there's something exciting about starting the day with a little food-induced glow. Don't worry, the ratios in this recipe won't set your tongue ablaze, but there's enough heat to make the *harissa's* presence known. If you'd prefer something more temperate, try cheddar cheese and bacon crumbs, or za'atar with a drizzle of honey, instead of the *harissa*. The exposed avocado flesh forms a little surface tension while baking, but don't be dismayed; the warm avocado is a delightful companion to the egg it houses. Avocado is a baking vessel of champions.

3 ripe-but-firm avocados

6 eggs, yolks and whites separated

3 teaspoons *harissa* (or chile paste of your choice)

2 garlic cloves, smashed into a paste with kosher salt

½ cup whole-milk Greek yogurt

serves
6

Preheat the oven to 425°. Halve and pit the avocados. With a spoon, scoop a larger circle around the hole where the pit was, approximately 2 inches in diameter. Reserve the scooped-out avocado flesh.

Arrange the avocado halves snugly in a baking dish, leaning them against the sides or each other so that they stay upright. Carefully place one egg yolk into the cavity of each avocado half, then add enough egg white to fill until it has nearly reached the top. Bake for 17 minutes (check the eggs occasionally, as the time may vary based on the intensity of your oven).

Cut the reserved avocado flesh into cubes, then place in a small bowl and toss with the *harissa*. In a second small bowl, mix the garlic paste with the yogurt until well combined.

Remove the avocados from oven, top each with some of the *harissa*-tossed avocado chunks and a dollop of garlic yogurt and serve.

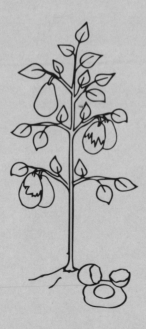

Roasted Broccoli, Brussels Sprouts & Avocado Salad with Tahini Dressing

When I lived in Paris during culinary school, I subsisted almost solely on the leftovers from class, all buttery, rich dishes of classic French cuisine. Thankfully, one night my friend Clotilde (of the food blog Chocolate & Zucchini) made me this combination of broccoli, Brussels sprouts and avocado. It was a necessary injection of vegetables. After that, I made it weekly and it served as my lifeline to an existence outside the classroom. I've modified it since then, and served it to friends countless times. (When you make this dish, you can consider yourself my friend, too.)

1 large head broccoli (or 2 small heads), cut into florets of equal size, stems discarded or saved for another use

2 overflowing cups brussels sprouts, trimmed and halved lengthwise

¼ cup olive oil

½ teaspoon kosher salt, plus more to taste

½ teaspoon freshly ground black pepper, plus more to taste

½ teaspoon red pepper flakes

¼ cup tahini

1 garlic clove, finely minced

1½ teaspoons fresh lemon juice

1½ teaspoons honey

1 avocado, cubed

2 teaspoons chopped cilantro

2 tablespoons chopped parsley

serves 4

Preheat the oven to 400°. In a large bowl, toss the broccoli florets and brussels sprouts with the oil. Add the salt, pepper and red pepper flakes and toss again. Spread on a baking sheet lined with parchment paper or a silicone baking mat. Roast the vegetables in the oven for 30 minutes, tossing them once halfway through cooking.

While the vegetables roast, make the dressing. In a medium bowl, whisk together the tahini, ¼ cup of water, the garlic, lemon juice and honey. Add a bit more water until you have a sauce-like consistency; you should be able to drizzle it.

After you've removed the vegetables from the oven, let them cool slightly. Gently toss the avocado chunks in with the roasted vegetables and season to taste with more salt and pepper, if needed. Transfer to a platter. Drizzle the tahini dressing over the top, sprinkle with the chopped herbs and serve.

Baked Avocado Rice

What is it about a bowl of flavorful rice that is so supremely satisfying? I am categorizing this dish as a side, but I've also eaten a bowl of this rice topped with a fried egg and happily called it dinner. It's an easy friend to almost anything you choose to pair it with: It's wonderful served on a bed of greens or as a side to grilled swordfish with avocado butter (page 33). The avocado brings a creaminess to this dish as it coats the rice, inviting spoonful after irresistible spoonful.

---

3 tablespoons olive oil

1 stalk lemongrass, trimmed, cut in half lengthwise and sliced

1 shallot, thinly sliced

2 garlic cloves, thinly sliced

1 teaspoon kosher salt

1 cup jasmine rice

1 avocado, mashed with a fork

2 teaspoons za'atar (see Note)

¼ cup fresh lime juice

Kosher salt and freshly ground black pepper

Sriracha, to taste

serves
4 to 6

Preheat the oven to 400°. Pour the oil into a Dutch oven and place it over medium-high heat. Once the oil is shimmering, add the lemongrass, shallot and garlic and stir for 45 seconds. Reduce the heat to medium low and stir in the kosher salt and the rice.

Add 2 cups of water and bring to a boil. As soon as it boils, give it another quick stir, then cover and transfer to the oven.

Bake for 30 minutes, or until the rice is al dente, then remove from the oven. Stir in the mashed avocado, za'atar and lime juice. Season with salt and pepper. Top with a drizzle of Sriracha and serve.

Note: If you have trouble finding za'atar, which is a common Middle Eastern spice, you can substitute it with this mixture: ½ teaspoon oregano, ½ teaspoon cumin, ½ teaspoon white sesame seeds, ¼ teaspoon kosher salt and ¼ teaspoon black pepper.

Warm Grain & Avocado Salad with Dates

I'm usually eating some version of this salad for dinner on any given weeknight—it's healthy and filling, with little treats (goat cheese, dates, and, of course, avocado) buried in the mix to lend a note of indulgence. Toasting the millet here brings out its nuttiness, but it's a totally different kind of nuttiness than what the avocado brings to the table. I think of avocado's nutty notes as those found in some organic butters, which are determined by the diet of the cow; it's subtle, but provides undeniable richness of flavor. Millet is my personal favorite grain in this dish, but by all means try other grains here; they'll all work. In the mood for more greens? Swap the grains for a bed of arugula and enjoy.

1 cup millet

Kosher salt and freshly ground black pepper

1 tablespoon olive oil

2 avocados, 1 mashed and 1 cubed, divided

3 Medjool dates, pitted and chopped

3 teaspoons sumac (see Note)

2 tablespoons mint leaves, chopped, plus mint sprigs for garnish

2 ounces goat cheese, crumbled, divided

⅔ cup blueberries, rinsed

serves 4 to 6

Preheat the oven to 375°. Spread the millet on a baking sheet and toast in the oven for 8 to 10 minutes, stirring the grains after 5 minutes and keeping an eye on them to make sure they don't burn. Remove the millet from the oven and let it cool. Put the toasted millet in a pot and add 2 cups of water and the kosher salt. Stir and place over medium-high heat. Bring to a boil, then reduce to a simmer and cover. Cook until the water is absorbed, about 15 minutes. Drizzle with the oil and stir.

In a medium bowl, combine the mashed avocado, dates and sumac. Toss the warm millet in with that mixture until well combined. Taste and season with salt and pepper, as needed. Mix in the chopped mint and three-quarters of the goat cheese (reserve the rest for garnish), then gently fold in the avocado cubes and blueberries. Sprinkle with the remaining goat cheese and add a few mint sprigs. Serve!

Note: If you can't find sumac (you can order it online if you can't find it near you), substitute with 2 teaspoons coriander and ½ teaspoon lemon zest mixed with 1 teaspoon paprika.

Leafy Greens with Avocado-Maple Vinaigrette

A good salad dressing goes far in my book, as it can make an otherwise "meh" assembly of vegetables totally irresistible. This vinaigrette is excellent not only with leafy greens, but also drizzled over sliced beefsteak tomatoes and mozzarella or with roasted veggies and quinoa for a packed lunch worth looking forward to.

For the vinaigrette:

½ large avocado or 1 small avocado, thoroughly mashed

1 tablespoon Grade A maple syrup (amber color, rich taste)

2 tablespoons fresh lemon juice

½ teaspoon Dijon mustard

1 garlic clove, made into a paste with kosher salt

1 tablespoon minced shallot

½ cup olive oil

Salt and freshly ground black pepper

For the salad:

1 bunch of your favorite leafy greens (i.e., spinach, kale, arugula, romaine, Bibb lettuce), chopped or torn

serves 4 to 6

Make the vinaigrette: In a small bowl, combine all the vinaigrette ingredients except for the oil and salt and pepper. Slowly add the oil in a thin stream, whisking quickly as you pour, to create an emulsion. Add the salt and pepper, to taste. Voila! Your vinaigrette is ready.

Make the salad: Place the leafy greens in a bowl and add 2 tablespoons of vinaigrette. Gently toss, then serve. Store the remaining vinaigrette in an airtight container in the refrigerator, where it will keep for up to two weeks.

Guacamole

The word *guacamole* is combination of the Spanish word *agua-cate*, which means "avocado," and *mole*, which means "a mixture." So, literally, guacamole is avocado mixed together with anything. Technically, this entire cookbook is full of guacamole recipes, but I couldn't let the more widely accepted definition of guacamole go untouched here. I'm sharing my lick-your-fingers-good basic guacamole recipe, plus some mix-in ideas to add more texture and appease your appetite, whatever it may be. Your guacamole isn't only a dip for tortilla chips; add it to soups, serve it with a meaty main dish or spoon it over rice.

2 large or 3 small avocados

½ large jalapeño pepper (or 1 small jalapeño pepper), finely chopped (remove the seeds before chopping if you want less heat)

¼ teaspoon kosher salt

1 tablespoon fresh lime juice

2 tablespoons finely diced white onion (about ¼ one small onion)

¼ teaspoon ground cumin

3 tablespoons chopped cilantro

2 garlic cloves, minced

serves **2**

In a medium bowl, mix all the ingredients together, mashing them until the mixture reaches your desired consistency—anywhere on the spectrum from rustic and chunky to velvety smooth. Add a pinch more salt if needed.

Guacamole mix-in inspiration:
Pineapple, mango, pomegranate seeds, cucumber, tomatoes, grapes, coconut, chipotle chiles, cooked tomatillos, pistachios, pecans, almonds, chorizo, bacon, blue cheese, feta cheese, mayonnaise.

Avocado Fries with Spicy Mayo

The county fair inspired this creation. (I've never said that before!) My fellow YouTuber Adrienne Stortz and I decided to do a "Fry-day Friday" video shoot, where, as an homage to fair food, we battered and fried whole whoopie pies (take THAT, fried Oreos!) and avocado slices. The avocado fries became one of the most-viewed videos on my YouTube channel, and for good reason. They're crunchy and golden on the outside, vibrantly green and creamy on the inside. Dipped in a spicy mayonnaise, these are even more addictive.

For the dipping sauce:

¼ cup mayonnaise

2 teaspoons Sriracha

1 teaspoon fresh lime juice

For the avocado fries:

1 quart vegetable oil (or other plain-tasting frying oil, such as peanut oil)

½ cup all-purpose flour

1 teaspoon ground cumin

1 egg

1 avocado, sliced lengthwise into 10 wedges

Kosher salt

makes 10 fries

Make the dipping sauce: In a small bowl, combine the mayonnaise, Sriracha and lime juice; set aside.

Make the fries: Pour the oil into a wok, cast-iron skillet or Dutch oven and place over high heat. (I prefer using a wok because the sloped sides make it easier to maneuver the avocado slices.)

In a small bowl, mix the flour and cumin together. In another small bowl, beat the egg.

Dip each avocado slice into the flour mixture, immerse it in the beaten egg, then return it to the flour mixture and coat well. Lay each battered avocado slice on a plate; prepare all the avocado slices before you begin frying them.

Carefully lower the avocado slices into the hot oil one at a time, minimizing splashing by placing one end of the avocado in the oil, then gently releasing it. Use a metal slotted spoon or a spider strainer to continuously move the avocado slices around in the oil.

Once the batter turns golden on all sides, about 3 minutes, remove the fries from the oil and drain on a paper towel–lined plate (which actually wicks away more oil than using a wire rack and does not make the fried avocado soggy, contrary to popular belief). Season with salt immediately.

Arrange the fries on a platter and serve with the dipping sauce.

White Bean & Avocado Soup

This is everything I want in a soup. First, it's not fussy: It takes 30 minutes to make from start to finish. It's great warm or chilled. It has a bisque-like consistency but doesn't need a roux or uncooked rice to act as thickener. Jalapeño gives it some kick, but it's so balanced by the other elements that even my grandma could handle a jalapeño (seeds removed) here. Eat the soup by itself, or top it with a dollop of garlic yogurt (page 15).

2 tablespoons olive oil

1 large yellow onion, roughly chopped

3 jalapeños, chopped (remove the seeds if you want a mild version)

3 large garlic cloves, roughly chopped

2 teaspoons kosher salt, plus more to taste

1 teaspoon freshly ground black pepper, plus more to taste

Two 15-ounce cans cannellini beans, drained and rinsed

2 cups vegetable broth

1 avocado, roughly chopped

1 packed cup fresh spinach, tough stems discarded

⅓ cup coconut milk

2 tablespoons fresh lemon juice

Fresh herbs such as parsley, chives or cilantro, for serving

serves 4 to 6

In a Dutch oven or heavy-bottomed saucepan, heat the oil over medium heat. Once the oil is shimmering, add the onion, jalapeños, garlic, salt and pepper; mix well. Cook for 3 minutes, until the mixture is fragrant and the onion begins to become translucent. Add the cannellini beans and stir. Add the vegetable broth and 2 cups of water. Bring the soup to a boil, then reduce to a simmer and cook for 10 minutes, until the vegetables are very soft. Remove the pan from the heat and stir in the avocado and spinach.

Ladle the soup into a blender or food processor (working in batches if necessary) and blend until smooth. Return the soup to the Dutch oven and stir in the coconut milk and lemon juice. Taste and season with salt and pepper, if desired. Serve the soup warm, or chill it in the refrigerator and serve it cold. I like to sprinkle any fresh leafy herbs I have in the fridge, such as parsley, chives, cilantro, etc., on top.

Avocado Cornbread

Trust me: I would never give you a recipe for dry cornbread. It's the worst. This loaf is super moist and has delightful depth of flavor. With each bite, you get a bit of sweetness from the maple syrup, salty crunch from the bacon and smooth nuttiness from avocado mixed into the batter, with bonus avocado chunks nested inside. Did I mention that it's downright fluffy too? Thank the avocado oil, which further plants the avocado flag securely in this cornbread.

4 strips bacon

1¼ cups cornmeal

¾ cup all-purpose flour

2 teaspoons baking soda

1 teaspoon kosher salt

2 tablespoons sugar

2 tablespoons butter, at room temperature

2 avocados, 1 mashed and 1 cubed, divided

1 cup buttermilk (see Note), well shaken

1 egg, beaten

1 tablespoon avocado oil (optional)

Scant ¼ cup maple syrup

Preheat the oven to 375°. In a cold 8-inch cast-iron skillet, arrange the bacon strips in an even layer, then place the pan over medium-low heat and cook the bacon, flipping occasionally, until crisp, about 8 minutes.

Transfer the bacon to a paper towel–lined plate and pour off all but 1 tablespoon of the bacon fat. Set the skillet aside.

In a medium bowl, combine the cornmeal, flour, baking soda, salt and sugar. In a large bowl, combine the butter and the mashed avocado. Slowly whisk in the buttermilk and egg. Then, bit by bit, whisk in the cornmeal mixture, followed by the avocado oil (if using). When it's well mixed, fold in the cubed avocado.

Pour the batter into the prepared skillet and bake for 40 minutes, until the center looks firm and a toothpick inserted in the middle comes out clean. Meanwhile, chop the bacon into small bits.

Let the cornbread cool in the pan for 10 minutes, then, using a knife or spatula, loosen the cornbread along the sides of the skillet. Invert onto a plate and tap the bottom of the skillet to help release the cornbread. Cut the cornbread into wedges. Drizzle the maple syrup over the wedges and sprinkle on the bacon crumbs. Serve warm.

Note: No buttermilk on hand? You can substitute 1 scant cup of milk and 1 tablespoon of white vinegar. Stir the milk and vinegar together and let stand for 15 minutes before using.

Coconut-Curried Avocado Noodles

Spinach, you are not the only green pasta party in town. Here, pureed avocado is mixed into fresh pasta dough, then cooked and bathed in a spicy coconut curry sauce. The color is only one aspect of avocado's role here. The natural fat in the avocado, bolstered with avocado oil, creates silky, supple, melt-in-your-mouth noodles. The sauce is addictive and has a kick that will leave your guests with a happily tingling tongue...until you break out the Avocado Pudding (page 36) to cool things down and round out the feast.

For the noodles:

1 avocado, cubed

1 tablespoon avocado oil

2 eggs

1 egg yolk

2 cups all-purpose flour, plus up to ½ cup for dusting and kneading

1 teaspoon kosher salt

serves 4 to 6

For the coconut curry sauce:

One 13.5-ounce can sweetened coconut milk

2 tablespoons curry powder

1 garlic clove, minced

Zest of 1 lemon

1 teaspoon red pepper flakes

2 tablespoons soy sauce

½ teaspoon kosher salt

2 teaspoons sugar

1 to 2 tablespoons cornstarch

Make the noodles: In a food processor, pulse the avocado until smooth, then add the avocado oil and continue blending. With the motor running on low, add the eggs, egg yolk and 1 tablespoon of water and mix well.

In a large bowl, mix the 2 cups of flour and the salt, then make a well in the center. Add the avocado and egg puree to the well, then, using a spoon, slowly work in the flour from the edges until the mixture is fully incorporated and a dough forms. As soon as the dough starts to form, transfer it to a floured surface and begin to knead, sprinkling with flour as you go to avoid the dough sticking to your hands. (The dough is a sticky one, so use up to ½ cup of flour during the kneading process, if necessary.) Knead for about 20 minutes, until the dough is smooth. Place the dough on parchment paper in a dry area of your kitchen and cover with a towel. Let sit for at least 5 minutes (or as long as a couple of hours) to allow the gluten network to relax.

While the dough is resting, make the coconut curry sauce: In a medium pot over medium-high heat, combine all the ingredients except the cornstarch and stir well.

A quick note on the texture of the sauce: Add only 1 tablespoon of cornstarch for a "normal" thick sauce, or add 2 tablespoons of cornstarch for a very thick sauce. (If you prefer it liquid-y, then don't add the cornstarch.)

In a small bowl, mix 1 or 2 tablespoons of cornstarch, depending on your preference, with a couple of tablespoons of water to make a cornstarch slurry. When the mixture in the pot comes to a boil, slowly whisk in the cornstarch slurry. You'll see the sauce thicken immediately. Reduce the heat to medium low and cook for another few minutes, whisking frequently. I prefer it to get to the consistency of gravy—but do what you like best. Keep the sauce warm while you finish making the pasta.

Cut the dough into four equal pieces. Flatten each quarter with your hands, then feed them through a pasta machine set to the narrowest gauge. Lay the sheets on a lightly floured piece of parchment paper and let dry for 5 minutes. Cut the sheets into your noodle size of choice— I prefer running them through my tagliatelle pasta machine attachment, but my fiancé likes it when I hand-cut them to make wider, uneven noodles. Once the noodles are cut, hang them over the sides of a large bowl and let dry for 10 minutes.

Bring a pot of salted water to boil and add a quarter of the fresh noodles. Cook for 3 minutes, then drain and shock in an ice-water bath for

1 minute. Repeat with the remaining noodles, cooking, draining and shocking in batches.

Drain the noodles and shake off any excess water. Divide the noodles among bowls, top with the sauce and serve.

Avocado Pesto with Zucchini Noodles

A few years ago, I made this avocado pesto so frequently—it was lunch or dinner multiple times a week—you'd think I was sprouting basil from my ears (if only!) and hiccuping avocados. I was inspired by my sister-in-law, Clare, who blends an avocado with her basil bounty as a way to stave off its brown-spotted fate (she hates an overripe avocado). This pesto pairs beautifully with raw zucchini noodles, and the combination offers a light meal for those sweaty, sticky days in the summer. In the wintertime, I like using buckwheat noodles. If you don't have a spiralizer, use a vegetable peeler to create thin zucchini ribbons.

½ cup packed basil leaves

1 avocado, cubed

¼ cup almonds

1 tablespoon nutritional yeast

3 tablespoons olive oil

2 teaspoons fresh lemon juice

¼ teaspoon red pepper flakes

½ teaspoon kosher salt

3 zucchinis, spiralized or peeled into ribbons

serves ·4·

Combine all of the ingredients except the zucchini in a food processor and process until the mixture is fully incorporated and reaches your preferred pesto consistency.

Place the zucchini noodles in a bowl and pour the pesto over them. Toss to coat and serve.

Chimichurri-Avocado Chicken Salad Sandwiches

Whenever I make this sandwich for friends and tell them it has no mayonnaise, they're dumbfounded. Such is the beauty of the avocado and its highly flavorful fat content; when it's squashed into a paste, it serves as a mayo-like binder. The mild flavor gets an energizing boost from the red pepper flakes and fresh parsley, which pushes it ahead of the more traditional school lunch fodder. You can substitute chicken breasts for the chicken thighs if you like, but beware, breasts are more prone to dry out. If you do swap out thighs for breasts, increase the olive oil to ½ cup.

4 boneless, skinless chicken thighs

⅓ cup olive oil

1 tablespoon white wine vinegar

1 avocado, quartered

1¼ packed cups parsley (about 1 bunch)

3 garlic cloves

2 teaspoons dried oregano

1 teaspoon red pepper flakes

½ teaspoon salt

½ teaspoon freshly ground black pepper

2 celery stalks, thinly sliced

4 to 6 slices artisan bread, lightly toasted

serves 4 to 6

Place the chicken in a large heavy-bottomed pot and cover with water by an inch. Bring to a boil, then reduce the heat to low, cover and simmer for 15 minutes. To check the chicken's doneness, cut into the thickest part of the thigh; the flesh should be opaque. Transfer the chicken to a paper towel–lined plate and let cool. Using your fingers or a fork, shred the thigh meat and refrigerate it until ready to use.

In a food processor, combine the oil, vinegar, avocado, parsley, garlic, oregano, red pepper flakes, salt and pepper and process until the mixture reaches a slightly textured sauce-like consistency. You'll have about 1 cup of the sauce, but you'll need only half of it to mix with the chicken. Save the rest of the sauce in a sealed container in the refrigerator and use within a week.

In a mixing bowl, toss the sauce with the shredded chicken until well coated. Stir in the sliced celery. Spoon it on the toast and serve.

Grilled Swordfish with Avocado Butter

Avocados already have an incredible buttery quality, so why not just take the common ground to the next step? The ratio of butter here is less than with most compound butters because, c'mon, avocado doesn't need *that* much help. You could even add less butter than I call for, although it won't spread over your dish quite as seductively. I love the avocado butter with oily fish, like swordfish, but it's also great on steak, or even simply smeared on a baguette!

---

1 avocado, quartered

4 tablespoons unsalted butter, softened

1 shallot, roughly chopped

1 garlic clove, roughly chopped

2 teaspoons mint, roughly chopped

¼ teaspoon finely grated lemon zest

2 teaspoons fresh lemon juice

2 teaspoons ground coriander

¼ teaspoon red pepper flakes

Salt and freshly ground black pepper

4 swordfish steaks (about 1 pound total, 4 to 6 ounces each)

¼ cup olive oil, plus more for greasing the grill

serves
·4·

In a food processor, combine the avocado, butter, shallot, garlic, mint, lemon zest and lemon juice, coriander, red pepper flakes and 1 teaspoon each of salt and pepper. Process until well incorporated. Scoop the mixture onto a piece of parchment paper and shape into a log. Roll the parchment paper around the mixture and refrigerate until chilled (about 4 hours). Once the butter has formed its log shape, remove it from the refrigerator and bring to room temperature.

Preheat a grill to medium heat and, using a brush, oil the grill grates. If your swordfish has been in the refrigerator, let it come to room temperature. Season each fillet with salt and pepper and coat with oil. Grill the swordfish for 3 minutes, then rotate it 90 degrees to create crosshatch grill marks (if you want to be fancy). Cook the swordfish for another 3 minutes. Turn the swordfish over and cook for another 3 to 5 minutes, or until the center is just cooked through. Remove the fish from the grill and top with a ½-inch-thick nub of the room-temperature butter. Keep the butter nearby—you'll want to continue slathering it on as you eat. Any extra compound butter will keep in the refrigerator, tightly sealed, for 2 weeks.

Avocado-Guava Hand Pies

Usually Internet commenters get a bad rap (looking at you, trolls), but I've been really lucky. I've made incredible kitchen discoveries through the comments section of my YouTube channel and Facebook page, including these traditional guava hand pies, which were recommended by a subscriber named Camila. Their sweetness relies on a puree of guava paste and sugar and pairs well with the savory, stringy mozzarella and buttery, soft avocado. With their crispy brûléed crust, the hand pies are as beautiful as they are delicious.

½ cup all-purpose flour, for dusting

14 ounces puff pastry (2 sheets), thawed

½ avocado, cubed

¼ pound fresh mozzarella cheese, shredded

¼ cup guava paste, cut into 1-inch-by-½-inch pieces

1 tablespoon butter, melted

¼ cup turbinado sugar

makes 8 pies

Preheat the oven to 375°. Line a baking sheet with parchment paper or a silicone baking mat.

Dust a work surface with flour and place one sheet of puff pastry on it. Using a rolling pin, roll out the pastry to flatten it, ensuring that it's equally thick the whole way around. Cut the pastry sheet into 8 equal-size rectangles. Repeat with the second sheet; you should have a total of 16 rectangles.

On half of the rectangles, place one avocado cube, a similar amount of mozzarella and one piece of guava paste. Cover those rectangles with the remaining pieces of pastry. Using a fork, seal each pair of pastry pieces together, making sure the filling is secure inside.

Arrange the hand pies on the prepared baking sheet and place in the freezer for 10 minutes (to allow the puff pastry to firm up again). Remove the pies from the freezer, brush with the melted butter and sprinkle with the turbinado sugar. Bake for 12 minutes, until the pastry is golden and the sugar turns a glistening brown. Let cool and enjoy!

Avocado Pudding

Food lovers from the Philippines represent the second largest group of viewers for my YouTube channel (the largest number live in the United States). Me and the Philippines, we're culinary soul mates. Avocados appear frequently in the cuisine and are commonly grown there on backyard trees; they have both green-skinned and purple-skinned varieties. Thanks to one of my fantastic Filipina viewers, Abbie, for this recipe. The avocado chocolate chips are not a part of the original recipe, but I couldn't resist including them because I love them that much.

4 ounces milk chocolate, broken into smaller pieces if not already in chunks

2 teaspoons avocado oil

2 avocados

2 bananas

One 14-ounce can sweetened condensed milk (or less, depending on your sweet tooth)

serves 4 to 6

In a metal bowl set over a saucepan filled with 2 inches of simmering water, melt the chocolate, stirring constantly. Remove the bowl from the heat and stir in the avocado oil. Line a baking sheet with parchment paper, then pour the melted chocolate over it, spreading it with an offset spatula to make an even layer. Freeze the chocolate until it's firm, then break it into raisin-size pieces. Return the chocolate to the freezer until you're ready to mix it into the pudding.

In a medium bowl, combine the avocados, bananas and condensed milk. Using a fork or potato masher, mash everything together well until the mixture is smooth. Add the raisin-size pieces of chocolate and stir until they're evenly distributed throughout the pudding. Refrigerate the pudding for at least 2 hours; it's ready to eat when it has cooled all the way through. If you use the entire can of condensed milk, the pudding will keep in your refrigerator, sealed, for 5 days. If you use less condensed milk, the pudding will brown and turn a bit quicker.

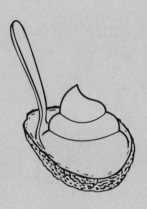

Black Sesame Cupcakes with Avocado-Cream Cheese Frosting

When I hosted some friends visiting from Beijing, I made a version of these cupcakes as muffins to nibble on sleepily with coffee in the morning. They were such a hit that I continued experimenting and came up with a combination to make it a real home run. I tinkered with the ratios to create a cupcake-like texture and velvety avocado–cream cheese frosting. From New York to China, these will put a smile on your guests' faces.

For the cupcakes:

1 cup all-purpose flour

1 tablespoon cocoa powder

1½ teaspoons baking powder

½ teaspoon kosher salt

½ cup (1 stick) unsalted butter, room temperature

¾ cup granulated sugar

2 eggs

2 teaspoons pure vanilla extract

¾ cup whole milk

2 tablespoons plus 1 teaspoon toasted black sesame seeds, divided

For the avocado–cream cheese frosting:

4 tablespoons (½ stick) unsalted butter, softened

2 ounces cream cheese, softened

1 avocado, roughly mashed

½ teaspoon pure vanilla extract

1 cup confectioners' sugar

makes 16 to 18

Preheat the oven to 350°. Grease 2 cupcake pans and 16 to 18 cupcake liners (I use coconut oil spray), and place the liners in the pan. (Greasing both the pans and the liners ensures easy removal and beautifully shaped cupcakes.)

Make the cupcakes: In a medium bowl, whisk together the flour, cocoa powder, baking powder and salt. In a separate, larger bowl, use an electric mixer to cream together the butter and sugar, then mix in the eggs, vanilla and milk. Slowly add the dry ingredients to the bowl with the wet ingredients and mix until just combined. Stir in 2 tablespoons of the toasted black sesame seeds. Pour the mixture into the prepared cupcake liners, filling each one to about half an inch from the top. Bake for 25 minutes, until a tester inserted into the center of a cupcake comes out clean. Remove the pans from the oven and place them on a wire rack or trivet. Let the cupcakes cool completely in the cupcake pans before removing.

Make the frosting: Using an electric mixer, cream the butter and cream cheese together. Add the avocado and vanilla and mix thoroughly. Add the confectioners' sugar bit by bit, mixing well until completely combined.

Top each cupcake with some frosting and sprinkle with the remaining teaspoon of black sesame seeds.

Unfrosted, the cupcakes will keep in an airtight container at room temperature for up to 1 week, and the frosting can keep in the refrigerator for 3 days, but will discolor more with each successive day due to oxidation.

Chocolate-Avocado Meringue Cookies

Meringue has always made me feel like a wizard in the kitchen with the whisk as my wand! Although it can be fun to whisk frenetically, I recommend using a handheld electric mixer or stand mixer with the whisk attachment for this. Chocolate and avocado is one of my favorite flavor pairings (if all the avocado-chocolate mousse recipes that took health food blogs by storm a few years ago are any indication of what's popular, others must also like the combo). Folding in the avocado and chocolate at the end is a nod to Italian meringue, which takes classic meringue one step further by adding cooked sugary syrup after whisking, which creates a meringue that's softer and more pliable than classically baked meringue.

¼ cup dark (65% cacao) chocolate chips

½ avocado, mashed until smooth

3 egg whites, at room temperature

¾ cup confectioners' sugar, divided

½ teaspoon pure vanilla extract

½ teaspoon cream of tartar

2 tablespoons cocoa powder

2 teaspoons cornstarch

1 tablespoon flaky sea salt

Preheat the oven to 300°. Line a baking sheet with parchment paper or a silicone baking mat.

In a metal bowl set over a saucepan filled with 2 inches of simmering water, or in a microwave (heating in 10-second increments), melt the chocolate. Let the chocolate cool to room temperature, about 10 minutes, then stir in the avocado. If it's cold in your kitchen, you'll want to keep this bowl over a double boiler with the heat turned off to prevent the mixture from hardening. But if your kitchen is warm, you should be good.

Using an electric or standing mixer with the whisk attachment, beat the egg whites on high for about 2 minutes, until soft peaks just begin to form. Gradually add ½ cup of confectioners' sugar, using a spatula to wipe down the sides of the bowl intermittently. Add the vanilla and cream of tartar and continue to beat until the meringue is thick and glossy and has stiff peaks, a couple minutes longer.

Sift the remaining ¼ cup of sugar and the cocoa and cornstarch together in a small bowl, then beat that into the meringue bowl until combined. Put the whisk attachment aside and gently fold in the melted chocolate-avocado combination with a spatula, stopping before it's fully incorporated; the mixture should look slightly marbled. If you overbeat here, it will cause the cookies to fall flat.

Spoon heaping tablespoons of the mixture onto the prepared baking sheet, spacing them evenly about ½ inch apart. Bake for 25 minutes, then turn off the oven but don't remove the baking sheet. Let the cookies sit in the warm oven for 1 hour. Remove the meringues from the oven and sprinkle a few grains of the sea salt over each cookie. These are best eaten the same day they're made, but if you're not serving them right away, store the meringues in an airtight container for up to 1 week.

Avocado Margaritas

In 2013 I visited Austin, Texas as part of the crowd that descended for the South by Southwest (SXSW) music, film and technology festival. Curra's Grill is a beloved establishment there, and for good reason. Its Mexican food was better than anything I can readily get in the Northeast, and the uber-creamy avocado margarita served there was enough to make me seriously consider moving down South. In fact, none of my other adventures at SXSW could hold a candle to this margarita; it was the highlight of my visit. Here's my version of it.

1 tablespoon kosher salt

⅛ teaspoon cayenne pepper

3 ounces tequila blanco

1½ ounces orange liqueur (such as Cointreau, Triple Sec, Dry Curaçao)

1½ ounces fresh lime juice

¾ ounce agave nectar

½ large avocado, cubed (a heaping ½ cup)

2 cups ice

makes 2

In a shallow dish that will fit the rim of a rocks glass, combine the salt and cayenne pepper. Add some water to another small shallow dish and dip the rim of the glass in the water. Dip the rim into the salt mixture and rotate until the rim is coated. Repeat with a second glass.

In a blender, combine the tequila, orange liqueur, lime juice, agave, avocado and ice. Blend until combined.

Pour the margarita mixture into the salt-rimmed glasses and serve.

Avocado Yogurt Smoothies

The basic iteration of this smoothie became a staple in my home because it saves ingredients on the brink of going bad (spinach, that last spoon or two of yogurt in the container) from being wasted. The task of nailing down a specific recipe for this cookbook proved to be a delicious challenge, and I love the results so much that I'm not inclined to return to my extemporaneous smoothie creations.

1 avocado

½ cup plain Greek yogurt

½ cup coconut milk

One ½-inch-by-1-inch piece of ginger (roughly the size of a thumb), peeled

1 cup packed spinach

2 dates, pitted

½ teaspoon pure vanilla extract

2 tablespoons agave nectar

1 teaspoon fresh lemon juice

1 cup ice cubes (4 ice cubes from a standard-size ice cube tray)

makes
—2—

In a blender or food processor, combine all the ingredients (place the ingredients in your machine in the order directed by the instruction manual, if specified) and puree until well incorporated and completely smooth. Pour into a large glass and serve.

Thank You!

Thank you to Short Stack Editions! To Nick and Kaitlyn for giving me the opportunity to put my avocado adoration into words, and for helping craft it into the book you now hold in your hands. To my dad for lending his editor's eye to my manuscript while it was just a jumble of thoughts in a Google doc, and to Dana Boals for her polishing tips. To my mom and the incredibly talented Erica Von Trapp for their insights while testing many of my recipes to make sure that anyone so inclined could recreate them with success. Obrigado to Jeremy for being my cheerful and grateful garbage disposal (with a discerning palate to boot!) throughout my storm of recipe testing.

Everyone ought to have a Connor in her life—he encourages me with unwavering support for any project I dive into, and this book was no exception. I am beyond thankful for his steadfastness and love.

Thanks to the fans of my QKatie videos! You have opened up the world to me, you bring a smile to my face daily, and I am so grateful to have you on my side. And to anyone who picked up this book, anyone willing to play around and have fun making delicious creations with your favorite foods, I am grateful. You're my kind of people.

—Katie Quinn

Share your Short Stack cooking experiences with us
(or just keep in touch) via:

 #shortstackeds   facebook.com/shortstackeditions

 @shortstackeds   hello@shortstackeditions.com

Colophon

This edition of Short Stack was printed by Stephen Gould Corp. in Richmond, Virginia on Mohawk Britehue Lime Green (interior) and Neenah Oxford White (cover) paper. The main text of the book is set in Futura and Jensen Pro, and the headlines are set in Lobster.

Available now at ShortStackEditions.com: